W9-BIH-865

Native American Library

NEZ PERCE
History and Culture

Helen Dwyer and Mary A. Stout

Consultant Robert J. Conley
Sequoyah Distinguished Professor at Western Carolina University

Gareth Stevens
Publishing

Please visit our website, **www.garethstevens.com**. For a free color catalog of all our high-quality books, call toll free 1-800-542-2595 or fax 1-877-542-2596.

Library of Congress Cataloging-in-Publication Data

Dwyer, Helen.
Nez Perce history and culture / Helen Dwyer and Mary A. Stout.
    p. cm. — (Native American library)
Includes index.
ISBN 978-1-4339-6678-1 (pbk.)
ISBN 978-1-4339-6679-8 (6-pack)
ISBN 978-1-4339-6676-7 (library binding)
1. Nez Percé Indians—History. 2. Nez Percé Indians—Social life and customs. I. Stout, Mary, 1954- II. Title.
E99.N5D89 2012
979.5004'974124—dc23

                                2011026004

New edition published in 2012 by
Gareth Stevens Publishing
111 East 14th Street, Suite 349
New York, NY 10003

First edition published 2005 by Gareth Stevens Publishing

Copyright © 2012 Gareth Stevens Publishing

Produced by Discovery Books
Project editor: Helen Dwyer
Designer and page production: Sabine Beaupré
Photo researchers: Tom Humphrey and Helen Dwyer
Maps: Stefan Chabluk

Photo credits: Corbis: pp 17, 22, 24; Getty Images: pp. 33 (Marilyn Angel Wynn/Nativestock.com), 34 (Marilyn Angel Wynn/Nativestock.com); Native Stock: pp. 10, 12, 20, 21 (bottom), 25, 26, 30, 31, 32, 35, 36, 37 (both), 39; North Wind Picture Archives: pp. 14 (both), 18 (top), 19; Peter Newark's American Pictures: pp. 11, 13, 15, 16, 18 (bottom), 21 (top), 23, 27; Shutterstock: pp. 5, 28 (Michaela Stejskalova), 29 (Nancy Bauer), 38 (LSqrd42); Wikimedia: pp. 7, 8 (F. M. Sargent).

Printed in the United States of America

CPSIA compliance information: Batch # CW12GS: For further information contact Gareth Stevens, New York, New York at 1-800-542-2595.

CONTENTS

Words that appear in the glossary are printed in **boldface** type the first time they appear in the text.

INTRODUCTION

The Nez Perces are a people of Idaho, Washington, and Oregon in the western United States. They are just one of the many groups of Native Americans who live today in North America. There are well over five hundred Native American tribes in the United States and more than six hundred in Canada. At least three million people in North America consider themselves to be Native Americans. But who are Native Americans, and how do the Nez Perces fit into the history of North America's native peoples?

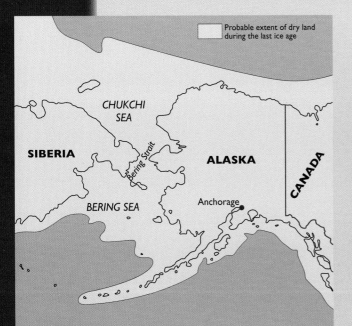

Siberia (Asia) and Alaska (North America) are today separated by an area of ocean named the Bering Strait. During the last ice age, the green area on this map was at times dry land. The Asian ancestors of the Nez Perces walked from one continent to the other.

THE FIRST IMMIGRANTS

Native Americans are people whose **ancestors** settled in North America thousands of years ago. These ancestors probably came from eastern parts of Asia. Their **migrations** probably occurred during cold periods called **ice ages**. At these times, sea levels were much lower than they are now. The area between northeastern Asia and Alaska was dry land, so it was possible to walk between the continents.

Scientists are not sure when these migrations took place, but it must have been more than twelve thousand years ago. Around that time, water levels rose and covered the land between Asia and the Americas.

The Cliff Palace at Mesa Verde, Colorado, is the most spectacular example of Native American culture that survives today. It consists of more than 150 rooms and pits built around A.D. 1200 from sandstone blocks.

By around ten thousand years ago, the climate had warmed and was similar to conditions today. The first peoples in North America moved around the continent in small groups, hunting wild animals and collecting a wide variety of plant foods. Gradually these groups spread out and lost contact with each other. They developed separate **cultures** and adopted lifestyles that suited their **environments.** The Nez Perce people lived in the Columbia River region. Several families came together in villages in winter but during the rest of the year, they moved around from place to place, hunting, fishing, and gathering seasonal food.

SETTLING DOWN

Although many tribes continued to gather food and hunt or fish, some Native Americans began to live in settlements and grow crops. Their homes ranged from underground pit houses and huts of mud and thatch to dwellings in cliffs. By 3500 B.C., a plentiful supply of fish in the Pacific Ocean and in rivers had enabled people to settle in large coastal villages from Alaska to Washington State. In the deserts of Arizona more than two thousand years later, farmers constructed hundreds of miles of **irrigation** canals to carry water to their crops.

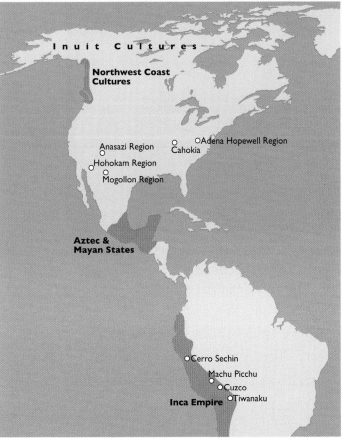

This map highlights some of the main early Native American cultures.

In the Ohio River valley between 700 B.C. and A.D. 500, people of the Adena and Hopewell cultures built clusters of large burial mounds, such as the Serpent Mound in Ohio, which survives today. In the Mississippi **floodplains**, the Native peoples formed complex societies. They created mud and thatch temples on top of flat earth pyramids. Their largest town, Cahokia, in Illinois, contained more than one hundred mounds and may have been home to thirty thousand people.

CONTACT WITH EUROPEANS

Around A.D. 1500, European ships reached North America. The first explorers were the Spanish. Armed with guns and riding horses, they took over land and forced the Native Americans to work for them. The Spanish were followed by the British, Dutch, and French, who were looking for land to settle and for opportunities to trade.

When Native Americans met these Europeans they came into contact with diseases, such as smallpox and measles, that they had never experienced before. At least one half of all Native Americans, and possibly many more than that, were unable to overcome these diseases and died.

Guns were also disastrous for Native Americans. At first, only the Europeans had guns, which enabled them to overcome native peoples in fights and battles. Eventually, Native American groups obtained guns and used them in conflicts with each other. Native American groups were also forced to take sides and fight in wars between the French and British.

Horses, too, had a big influence in Native American lifestyles, especially on the Great Plains. Some groups became horse breeders and traders. People were able to travel greater distances and began to hunt buffalo on horseback. Soon horses became central to Plains trade and social life. The Nez Perces acquired horses in the 1700s and soon adopted the buffalo-hunting lifestyle of Plains tribes. They began to breed horses themselves and trade them with other Native Americans.

At the end of the 1700s, people of European descent began to migrate over the Appalachian Mountains, looking for new land to farm and exploit. By the middle of the nineteenth century, they had reached the west coast of North America. This expansion was disastrous for Native Americans. Settlers arrived on Nez Perce land in the 1840s.

A late nineteenth-century image of two Nez Perces with an Appaloosa horse. The Appaloosa breed of horse was developed by the Nez Perces.

Chief Joseph of the Wallowa Valley Nez Perce and his family in Fort Leavenworth, Kansas, around 1878. The Nez Perces who surrendered in 1877 were taken to Kansas at first then moved to Oklahoma. In 1885, the surviving Nez Perce either returned to their reservation in Idaho or, like Chief Joseph, were sent to the Colville Reservation in Washington State.

RESERVATION LIFE

Many native peoples were pressured into moving onto **reservations**. The biggest of these reservations later became the U.S. state of Oklahoma. Native Americans who tried to remain in their homelands were attacked and defeated.

The Nez Perces gave up much of their land in return for a reservation in Idaho, but when the size of this reservation was reduced, some Nez Perces refused to accept. A war against the United States ended in defeat for the Nez Perce in 1877.

New laws in the United States and Canada took away most of the control Native Americans had over their lives. They were expected to give up their cultures and adopt the ways and habits of white Americans. It became a crime to practice their traditional religions. Children were taken from their homes and placed in **boarding schools**, where they were forbidden to speak their native languages.

Despite this **persecution**, many Native Americans clung on to their cultures through the first half of the twentieth century. The Society of American Indians was founded in 1911 and its campaign for U.S. citizenship for Native Americans was successful in 1924. Other Native American organizations were formed to promote traditional cultures and to campaign politically for Native American rights.

THE ROAD TO SELF-GOVERNMENT

Despite these campaigns, Native Americans on reservations endured **poverty** and very low standards of living. Many of them moved away to work and live in cities, where they hoped life would be better. In most cases, they found life just as difficult. They not only faced **discrimination** and **prejudice** but also could not compete successfully for jobs against more established ethnic groups.

In the 1970s, the American Indian Movement (AIM) organized large protests that attracted attention worldwide. They highlighted the problems of unemployment, discrimination, and poverty that Native Americans experienced in North America.

The AIM protests led to changes in policy. Some new laws protected the civil rights of Native Americans, while other laws allowed tribal governments to be formed. Today tribal governments have a wide range of powers. They operate large businesses and run their own schools and health care.

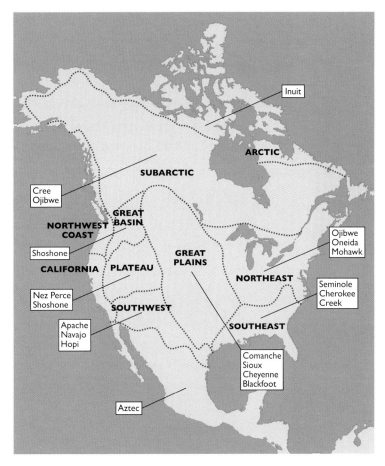

This map of North America highlights the main Native American cultural groups, along with the smaller groups, or tribes, featured in this series of books.

Chapter 1

LAND AND ORIGINS

Today, the Nez Perces can show you two hills near Kamiah, Idaho, that they believe are the Iltswewitsix's heart and liver (see page 11).

THE LAND OF THE NEZ PERCES

The Nez Perces today number about three thousand. Some still live in their traditional lands in northeastern Oregon, while others live throughout Washington, Oregon, and Idaho.

NEZ PERCE ORIGIN STORY

No one knows exactly how the Nez Perce and other Indian tribes got to North America. Like many Native groups, however, the Nez Perces explain their beginnings in an origin story.

The Nez Perces roamed throughout the Columbia River Valley in present-day Oregon, Washington, and Idaho. Their territory originally consisted of approximately 26,500 square miles (69,000 square kilometers).

10

According to this story, before there were people in the world, the animals, including Coyote, could talk and act like humans. One day a huge monster called Iltswewitsix began eating everything in sight. Coyote tied himself to the earth, hoping Iltswewitsix wouldn't eat him up with everything else, but the monster found him. Coyote knew the monster could easily eat him, so he quickly jumped down Iltswewitsix's throat. He went to the monster's heart, took out his stone knife, and began to cut its body up into pieces. Then he threw the pieces all over the land, creating many different tribes.

When he was done, Coyote realized that no tribe was in the Kamiah Valley in Idaho. Coyote shook some drops of the monster's blood off his fingers and made the last and best tribe, the Nimi'ipuu, or Real People, as the Nez Perces call themselves, right where he stood.

Some of the Nez Perce designs for beading and clothing were borrowed from the Plains Indian cultures. Sometimes, the Nez Perce people wore decorated hide shirts, pants, and dresses and beaded beautiful ornaments for their horses.

The Nez Perce Language

Scientists can tell from the Nez Perce language that they have always lived near the valleys of the Columbia River. The language spoken by the Nez Perce people is also called Nez Perce. In 1994, only thirty people spoke Nez Perce well, but today young people are studying the language.

Nez Perce	Pronunciation	English
mamin	mah-min	Appaloosa horse
qoqalx	kokah-lks	buffalo
qemes	ka-mas	camas lily
miyoxat	miyo-ksaht	chief
cuyem	tsoo-yam	fish
lewliks	la-wliks	salmon
timanit	timah-nit	berries

Chapter 2

HISTORY

LIFE BEFORE THE EUROPEANS

Of the many tribes living in the mountainous West, the Nez Perce Nation was at one time the largest and most powerful. The tribe began as a group of separate bands fishing, hunting, and gathering food in their own area.

RELATIONSHIPS WITH OTHER TRIBES

Once the Nez Perces started using horses in the 1700s, probably getting them from the Plains Indian tribes, the animals became an important part of their lifestyle. With the horse, they became better hunters and began to go on long buffalo hunts with other tribes on the Plains. The Nez Perces became famous for their fine horses, as they began to raise and train the animals for trade.

Names for the Nez Perces

Because of their blue face paint, some early traders called the Nez Perces "blue mud Indians."

During their early history, the Nez Perce people were called by different names depending upon who was talking about them. The Arikaras used a name meaning "bone across the nose." The Bannocks and Shoshones called them "couse eaters" and "couse people," referring to a food they ate, now called biscuitroot. The Pawnees called them "cut bangs" because of the men's hairstyle. The French called them, and a number of other tribes, the Nez Perce, which means "pierced nose" and refers to the shell ornaments they supposedly wore in their noses. Today, the Nez Perces say their ancestors never pierced their noses and that this name is a mistake.

Using horses, Nez Perce men were able to travel to the plains of Montana to hunt buffalo with the Flathead Indians. They also hunted other large game animals such as deer, moose, bears, elks, and mountain goats.

Over time, the Nez Perces built a trading empire. They traded with the Sioux, Crow, and Flathead tribes living east of them on the Plains. To the west, the Chinook, Walla Walla, and Palouse made good trading partners near the Pacific coast. The Nez Perces traded horses, bows, and woven baskets for these other tribes' canoes, hides, and flints.

LEWIS AND CLARK: EARLY CONTACT

Sent by President Thomas Jefferson, Meriwether Lewis and William Clark led an **expedition** to map and explore a large part of North America, meeting some of the Nez Perce people in 1805. The Nez Perces fed Lewis and Clark's weak and hungry group, helped them make canoes, and guided them toward the Pacific Ocean. In return, Lewis and Clark gave the Nez Perces gifts of cloth, ribbons, and peace medals.

Later meetings with European-Americans did not go so well for the Nez Perces. In 1836, a Christian minister, Henry Spalding, and his wife, Eliza, established a **Presbyterian mission** at Lapwai in what is now Idaho. Spalding tried to change the Nez Perces'

A Welcoming People

Lewis and Clark wrote about the Nez Perce people in their journals in 1805. Lewis described the Nez Perces: "I think we can justly affirm, to the honor of this people, that they are the most **hospitable**, honest and sincere people that we have met with in our voyage." This was a big compliment, because Lewis and Clark met about fifty different Native American tribes on their expedition across North America.

The diaries of Lewis and Clark, written from 1804 to 1806, contain the earliest written information about Nez Perce and many other Native American peoples.

White **officials** met with Native American chiefs at **treaty councils** to settle disagreements between the Native Americans and whites.

lifestyle, including their religion. In 1847, some of the Nez Perces told the Spaldings to stop interfering with their way of life, and they attacked the mission, but no one was hurt.

Settlers followed the **missionaries**, bringing their families in covered wagons on the Oregon Trail to live on lands that had been the home of the Nez Perce people. The settlers also brought diseases, such as smallpox and measles, that

Many pioneer families packed up their belongings and came west in wagons because they had heard that land was available. Many didn't realize that Native American peoples already lived on the land; some did not care.

killed many Nez Perces between 1846 and 1847. Without asking or paying the Nez Perce people, the settlers took the Nez Perces' traditional lands for their own.

THE "THIEF TREATY"

Governor Isaac Stevens was placed in charge of the new Northwest Territory, which included Nez Perce lands. He called the Walla Walla Treaty Council in 1855, where the Nez Perces met with him and agreed to give up much of their land in exchange for a 13-million-acre (5-million-hectare) reservation where they would be left to live in peace.

Governor Stevens made a new treaty in 1863 that cut the Nez Perce reservation to one-tenth of its original size, giving away all of the southern lands, including the Wallowa Valley. Chief Joseph and the bands that lived in the Wallowa Valley refused to sign the new treaty. However, Governor Stevens convinced other Nez Perce men to sign the treaty, which is today called the "Thief Treaty."

In 1861, miners discovered gold on the Nez Perce reservation. Ignoring the treaty, both settlers and miners moved into Nez Perce territory. Then they asked the government to protect them from the Nez Perces and to make the Natives move out!

NEZ PERCE WAR OF 1877: BEGINNINGS

At first, Chief Joseph and the other bands refused to leave their home. In May 1877, however, General Oliver Otis Howard said that the Nez Perce people must leave the Wallowa Valley and move onto the smaller Nez Perce reservation at Lapwai, Idaho, or the army would come after them.

I have heard about a bargain, a trade between some of these Indians and the white men concerning their land. But I belong to the land out of which I came. The Earth is my mother.

Toohoolhoolzote,
Nez Perce chief, 1877

The Nez Perce chiefs finally decided to move to the Lapwai Reservation because they did not want to fight the U.S. Army. Three angry young warriors raided a settlement, however, and killed four white men. Realizing this meant war, the Nez Perces fled to White Bird Canyon. The U.S. Army followed the Nez Perces to White Bird Canyon in 1877 and attacked them, but the Nez Perce warriors badly beat the army. The Nez Perce War had begun.

DEATH AT BIG HOLE

After the White Bird Canyon battle, the Nez Perces traveled east over the Bitterroot Mountains (part of the Rocky Mountain chain) to join with the Crow tribe. More than 1,900 soldiers came after the fewer than 250 Nez Perce warriors and 500 women and children. The Nez Perces camped at Big Hole, Montana, believing that the army would not follow them.

U.S. troops surprised the Nez Perces, however, and killed many of them, mostly women and children, at the Battle of Big Hole. When the Crow people refused to help them, the Nez Perces continued running, this time north toward Canada. The Nez Perce people knew that the army couldn't cross the border into Canada. General Howard kept following the Nez Perces, but his troops couldn't catch them. Instead, Howard asked Colonel Nelson Miles to take his troops ahead of the fleeing Nez Perces and cut them off in northern Montana.

On June 17, 1877, the Nez Perces defeated two companies of U.S. soldiers and some volunteers in White Bird Canyon, killing thirty-four. Led by Chief Joseph's brother, Ollokot, and White Bird, another Nez Perce chief, the Nez Perces had only a couple of wounded men.

General Oliver Otis Howard and his troops chased the Nez Perces for several months but could not catch up with them.

SURRENDER AND EXILE

The tired and hungry Nez Perces made camp at a creek near the Bears Paw Mountains in Montana, only 40 miles (64 kilometers) from the Canadian border. General Miles's troops reached them and attacked, killing many, so the Nez Perces agreed to surrender if they could return to the Lapwai Reservation. Some of the Nez Perces slipped away that night and crossed the border to join Sioux leader Sitting Bull's camp in Canada, but many stayed with Chief Joseph and surrendered.

Despite the agreement with General Miles, other army generals ignored the terms of the surrender and sent 431 Nez Perces to Fort Leavenworth, Kansas. In 1878, after much illness and death, they were moved to Indian Territory in present-day Oklahoma. In that hot and humid country, many Nez Perce people became ill with **malaria**.

At his surrender, Chief Joseph said, "Hear me, my chiefs, I am tired. My heart is sick and sad. From where the sun now stands, I will fight no more forever."

In 1895, a law called the Dawes Severalty Act allowed the Lapwai Reservation to be divided into little pieces and given to all the Nez Perce families; leftover land was sold. Thus tribal lands shrank again. The Nez Perce people who had converted to Christianity were in charge of the reservation and encouraged everyone to live a Euro-American lifestyle.

In 1885, exile finally ended for Chief Joseph's people. Although 431 Nez Perces surrendered in 1877, only 268 left Oklahoma in 1885. Some returned to Lapwai, the Nez Perce Reservation in Idaho, but Chief Joseph and his warriors were sent to the Colville reservation in present-day Washington State, where their **descendants** still live today.

> I think that, in his long career, Joseph cannot accuse the Government of the United States of one single act of justice.
>
> *Lieutenant [first name unknown] Wood, who had heard Chief Joseph's surrender speech*

A CULTURE SURVIVES

For many years, the Nez Perce people didn't pay attention to their tribal history or political issues. In 1923, however, under the leadership of James Stuart, the Nez Perce Home and Farm Association was founded. This group focused on Nez Perce tribal issues and in 1948 became the Nez Perce Tribal Executive Committee. During that same year, the old Lapwai Reservation became the Nez Perce Nation, governed by the executive committee as it is today. Since the 1960s, the Nez Perce tribe has tried to revive its traditional culture and expand its tribal lands.

TRADITIONAL WAY OF LIFE

Chapter 3

CYCLES OF LIFE

Before the mid-1800s, the Nez Perces lived in small bands and moved to follow the food that was available each season. In the spring, salmon swam up the rivers to lay eggs, where the Nez Perces caught them, using spears, nets, lines, hooks, and traps. They ate some of the fish and dried the rest to preserve it for the winter. Using snowshoes to hunt in the winter and spring, the Nez Perces hunted elk, moose, deer, rabbit, squirrel, duck, and grouse year-round.

In summer, the Nez Perces would travel to the mountains, where hunting was more important than fishing. The women gathered roots, greens, and berries. Camas root (lily bulbs) was the most important food, but bitterroot, couse (biscuitroot), wild onions, wild carrots, huckleberries, and chokecherries were all gathered. Women used sticks to dig up the roots and harvest them.

The permanent winter home of the Nez Perce people was the longhouse, which could be more than 100 feet (30 meters) long and shelter many families. An **A-frame** constructed over a long oblong

Its bright blue star-shaped flower makes the camas lily plant easy to spot. The bulbs are gathered and baked in a pit for three days with wood, bear grass, and moss.

The Nez Perce people began to use the tepee after trading with the Plains Indians. Made with wooden poles, the tepee was covered by **tule** mats, bison skins, or later on, canvas.

hole supported the roof and walls, which were hung with woven mats. Most Nez Perce bands used tepees for temporary homes when they traveled in the summer. They borrowed this idea from the Plains Indians.

The Nez Perces wore clothing made of the **hides** of deer, elk, and buffalo. Fringes, beads, quills, paint, and other things, like elk teeth, often decorated the shirts and leggings worn by the men and the loose dresses worn by the women. Both men and women wore moccasins made from hides.

Horses

Because horses helped so much in daily life, the Nez Perces valued them highly. Men used them for hunting and trained them for warfare, while both men and women rode horses to travel and used them to carry heavy loads. By picking only the best horses to have **offspring**, the Nez Perce tribe raised horses known for their speed and **endurance**.

Nez Perce villages were made up of several related families. Headmen were often chosen because their fathers were also chiefs or because they were highly respected.

LEADERSHIP

Small bands of Nez Perce people gathered in villages near streams where fish and water were available. Villages contained several families and were led by a headman, usually the oldest active man. While the headman was a spokesman for the village and solved disagreements, the village council, which included the male heads of all of the families, made most of the decisions that affected each village. Since the Nez Perces were made up of many different bands, they didn't really have a chief for the whole tribe.

The Nez Perce leaders were powerful because they could convince people to respect and follow them. They did not give orders but rather led by example and **persuasion**. If they were fair, honest, and generous and their lives provided a good model for the young to follow, people admired them.

Usually the headmen were peace chiefs, known for their wisdom, concern for people, and **eloquent** speech. However, other village leaders were war chiefs — brave, experienced warriors who led the men in battle. Sometimes the headmen were **medicine men**.

Chief Joseph (1832–1904)

During the Nez Perce War, many bands of the Nez Perce joined together, and Chief Joseph became their spokesman and unofficial chief.

Born in the Wallowa Valley in present-day Oregon, Chief Joseph was the son of Old Joseph, also a chief. When his father died in 1871, Joseph became the peace chief and his brother Ollokot became war chief. Both tried to remain peaceful and promised their father before his death that they would not sell the Wallowa Valley.

After treaty disagreements with the U.S. government, Chief Joseph, his people, and other bands traveled over 1,600 miles (2,600 km) and fought fourteen battles before they surrendered in 1877. Chief Joseph's wife died in the Battle at Big Hole, and Ollokot died in the Battle at Bears Paw Mountains.

An **accomplished** speaker, Joseph made some of his best speeches after his surrender. He finished his life on the Colville Reservation in Washington State and never saw the Wallowa Valley again. When he died, a white doctor wrote as the cause of death, "a broken heart."

CHILDREN AND TEENS

Babies were born in a small, separate "women's house." The mother was helped during birth by her own mother and other women. Young children spent most of their time with their grandparents, who taught them basic household tasks and told them stories. At about age three, they also began to participate in food-gathering activities, helping their relatives hunt, fish, dig for roots, or gather berries.

When boys became teenagers, they were often sent out alone to seek **visions** and find their helping spirit, or *wyakin*. Girls could undertake a vision quest, too, but they also had a special ceremony when they became adults at about age twelve or thirteen. They stayed alone in a hut for a week until they were welcomed back to the village with gifts to take their place as women ready for marriage.

Families often arranged those marriages. If both families felt that the match were a good one, the young people began living together. After a ceremony and gift exchange was completed, the young people were officially married.

After birth, babies were bound into **cradleboards** so they could be carried until they began to walk.

RITUALS FOR THE DEAD

As people grew older, they commanded more respect, power, and wealth in the tribe. When someone died, the death was publicly announced, and the female relatives began to cry and wail. The body was washed, painted, and dressed in new clothes. It was buried the day after death occurred, and the grave was marked with a stake. A medicine man performed a ceremony so that the ghost of the dead person would not haunt the living, and people avoided the grave afterward. Then the relatives hosted a feast and gave away the belongings of the dead person according to his or her wishes.

Nez Perce women decorated clothing, moccasins, and cradleboards with porcupine quills and colorful beadwork.

A Nez Perce Childhood

A typical Nez Perce child would wake before dawn and take a bath in a nearby stream. Often, a relative would lecture the children about proper behavior. Then girls would go with their grandmothers or other relatives to learn about gathering roots and berries, making meals, and sewing and decorating clothing. Boys went to their grandfathers or other male relatives to learn how to ride horses, fish, and hunt. When a young boy killed his first animal by himself or a young girl dug her first batch of roots at about age six, a ceremony was held. The family celebrated this accomplishment, and an important hunter would eat the boy's meat or a respected gatherer would eat the girl's roots.

TRADITIONAL BELIEFS

As recorded in the nineteenth century, the Nez Perces believed that all living things had spirits. They tried to live in harmony with the mountains, trees, rivers, and animals and respect these things' spirits. Through dreams and visions, people received power from spirits and communicated with them. Having **supernatural** power was important to the Nez Perce

Next to a river or stream, the Nez Perce created a hot bath, cold bath, and sweat lodge, which was built like a small dome.

Vision Quest

In the nineteenth century, when a Nez Perce teenager was ready, relatives took him or her to a place in the wilderness away from camp. They left the teenager there for three days and nights with a blanket. The teenager had no weapons or food and would build a fire for warmth at night and fast. The teenager was on a vision quest to discover the source of his or her power in the form of a helping spirit, or *wyakin*. Helping spirits could be from the trees, mountains, rivers, stars, or animals (as represented by the eagle claws shown here). At some point during the quest, in a dream or a vision, the teenager's special spirit would come and teach a power song. This spirit would stay with the seeker for the rest of his or her life, protecting the person.

way of life. Young people went on vision quests to discover a being known as their spirit helper and to explore how its supernatural power could be helpful.

The people who gained the most power from their spirit helpers were the tribe's medicine men and women. They could cure sick people, affect the weather, or predict the future of a hunting or war party. They also helped others find their spirit helpers and were in charge of the tribe's dances and ceremonies.

THE DREAMERS

The Nez Perces who followed these traditional beliefs were known as "Dreamers." Often, the Dreamers and the Christian Nez Perces disagreed on matters. Many Dreamers didn't sign the Thief Treaty in 1863 and fought in the Nez Perce War, while the Christian Nez Perces became the "treaty Indians" who lived

Jason, a Nez Perce medicine man. Nineteenth-century medicine men and women were important and respected in Nez Perce society.

on the Lapwai Reservation. Today, the Seven Drums Religion of the Nez Perce people recognizes and follows the traditional beliefs of the Dreamers.

Porcupine and Coyote

Just like stories told by many other tribes, Nez Perce stories feature Coyote and other animals as partly human beings, who spend much of their time trying to outwit each other. In this story, Porcupine and Coyote quarrel over food.

One day, Porcupine was walking by the river and saw several buffalo feeding on the other side. Cunningly, he called the largest buffalo over in a friendly way and asked for help to reach the far bank of the river. The buffalo walked over and offered to take Porcupine on his back. Porcupine said that he would prefer to ride holding on to the buffalo's underside, and when he reached the far side of the river, he stabbed the buffalo in the chest and killed him.

Then Porcupine realized that his knife was not sharp enough to cut the meat up. To add to his problems, Coyote arrived with a

When this story was first told, massive herds of buffalo roamed over the grasslands of North America. Although buffalo eat only plants, they can be very dangerous animals. If one charges, its huge head, and long horns, can easily crush humans or toss them into the air.

In reality, the North American Porcupine never eats buffalo. Most of its food comes from trees and other plants, mainly tree bark, conifer needles, twigs, roots, and berries.

sharp knife. "Whoever can jump over the buffalo can use the knife and eat all the buffalo," Coyote said, and immediately jumped over the body. Porcupine tried his hardest, but he couldn't jump that high. Then Coyote cut Porcupine in the head with his sharp knife, and Porcupine fell to the ground and pretended to be dead.

Coyote dropped his knife and ran off to fetch all his family to share in the feast. When he had gone, Porcupine got up, cut up the meat, and carried it into a tree. There he began to eat. When the Coyote family arrived they looked everywhere for the buffalo. Eventually Porcupine began laughing at them. Coyote saw him and begged for some scraps of meat. Porcupine thought for a moment, then he said: "Stand together under the tree and I will throw some meat down." When the Coyote family were all together under the tree, Porcupine dropped the buffalo's head on top of them, killing them all. And so, Porcupine was free to eat his meal in peace.

Chapter 4

NEZ PERCE LIFE TODAY

CONTEMPORARY NEZ PERCE

The old Lapwai Reservation in Idaho, which today is known as the Nez Perce Nation, covers about 750,000 acres (303,644 hectares) in five counties in north-central Idaho. The major towns on the reservation are Lapwai and Kamiah.

Many Nez Perce people live a typical American lifestyle. The tribe provides jobs and also works to make Nez Perce culture and language available to the young people. An elected nine-person committee, the Nez Perce Tribal Executive Committee, governs the reservation's tribal affairs.

The tribe farms over 37,000 acres (15,000 ha) of land, with wheat as the main crop. As well as harvesting timber and mining limestone on the reservation, the tribe owns a chain of grocery stores.

There are three thousand members of the Nez Perce tribe today. Of these, sixteen hundred live on the reservation.

The Nez Perces have built two **casinos** near Lewiston and Kamiah on their reservation in Idaho that have provided the tribe with funds and been popular with tourists. Some state officials have tried to limit or close the casinos to stop gambling in Idaho but have so far been unsuccessful.

Young Horseman Project

Nez Perce youths, ages fourteen to twenty-one, are being asked to join the Young Horseman Project to learn how to raise and train horses to bring back the Nez Perce tradition of fine horses. After the Nez Perce War, when Chief Joseph and his people surrendered, thousands of horses were taken from the tribe and never returned. In 1994, the Nez Perce Tribal Council accepted gifts of Appaloosa mares from a southwestern rancher and four Akhal-Teke stallions from a German executive. Appaloosas were originally bred by the Nez Perces in the 1700s, while Akhal-Teke horses come from Central Asia. Now the Nez Perces have **bred** a new type of horse, called the Nez Perce Appaloosa, which is the offspring of the Akhal-Teke stallion and the western Appaloosa mare.

The Nez Perce Trail

The U.S. Army chased the Nez Perces for 1,600 miles (2,600 km) through four states for four months before the Nez Perces surrendered near Havre, Montana, on October 5, 1877. In 1986, Congress decided that the route that Chief Joseph's people followed from the Wallowa Valley in Oregon to Bears Paw Mountains in Montana should be a national trail, called the Nez Perce National Historic Trail. In 1997, highway markers were built in all the states through which the trail runs.

Covering much of the land near to the trail, the Nez Perce National Historic Park contains 38 sites of importance to the Nez Perce people. These include many of the battlefields, Chief Joseph's grave, and natural landscape features that are of importance in Nez Perce stories. A park visitor center in Spalding, Idaho, contains a Nez Perce museum.

This highway into the Wallowa Valley is the beginning of the Nez Perce National Historic Trail. Using today's roadways, this historic trail, which is 1,170 miles (1,885 km) long, closely follows the route taken by the Nez Perces in 1877.

LIFE ON THE COLVILLE RESERVATION

Descendants of Chief Joseph, Yellow Wolf, Yellow Bull, and the other captured warriors still live on the Colville Reservation in Washington State. They gather to sing, dance, and pray. Many participate in the Seven Drums Religion, which follows traditional Nez Perce beliefs.

These Nez Perces are part of the Colville Confederated Tribes community. The Colville Confederated Tribes consist of the Colville, Nespelem, San Poil, Lake, Palus, Wenatchi, Chelan, Entiat, Methow, Southern Okanogan, Moses Columbia, and Nez Perces of Chief Joseph's band. Together, they serve on the tribal council and work with their neighbors for the good of the entire reservation.

A Nez Perce woman in traditional dress and her Appaloosa horse prepare to ride part of the Nez Perce Trail in honor of Chief Joseph and his band.

Nez Perce spiritual leader Horace Axtell drums and sings traditional songs at a gathering in the Wallowa Valley. Axtell is one of the few Nez Perce language speakers left and regularly performs songs and prayers in the language.

CHANGES IN EDUCATION

Today, although a large number of students fail to graduate from school, many young Nez Perces see a good education as important for gaining employment later. Some adult Nez Perce who feel they missed out on education at school are now taking part in distance learning courses in Lapwai and Kamiah. These courses cover the subjects they missed at school. They are provided by more distant colleges such as Lewis-Clark State College in Lewiston, Idaho, and the Northwest Indian College in Bellingham, Washington State. If they graduate, these adults usually go on to four-year college courses.

Nez Perce children are encouraged to learn about their history by visiting their historic sites. Preserving the language, however, is much more difficult, even though it is taught in schools. Only about twenty fluent Nez Perce speakers are left, and only a very few of them help teach the language.

> We don't have that many elders left. We need to hear our elders more. We're taping as much as we can. Our language is in danger of not existing. We're submerged in English. We're drowning in English.
>
> *Angel Sobotta*
> *Nez Perce language*
> *coordinator*

HEALTH AWARENESS

The Nez Perce tribal government runs many health campaigns, such as disease prevention and weight management. It also produces newsletters and posters on health issues. Now the Nez Perces are becoming more aware of what causes common health problems, such as diabetes and heart disease, and what they can do to improve their health. The tribe has recently built the Nimiipuu Health Center in Lapwai, which includes a fitness room with up-to-date exercise equipment.

POWWOWS

The Nez Perce tribe sponsors a number of annual powwows, dances, and memorials that feature music, drumming, dancing, crafts, and, of course, food. During the first weekend in March at Lapwai, the E-Peh-Tas Powwow features competitive war dancing, while the Mata'Lyma Powwow and Root Feast is held in Kamiah during the third weekend of May with traditional dancing. The Warriors Memorial Powwow during the third weekend of June honors Chief Joseph and his warriors. In August, the Nez Perce War Memorial (Big Hole) is held, and the Bears Paw War Memorial is in October.

At the Nez Perce Tamaliks Wallowa Band powwow in Oregon, people wear traditional clothing, eat traditional foods, and perform traditional dances.

During a powwow, tribal members and guests come together to celebrate Nez Perce history and tradition. The Nez Perce people like to share their culture and teach others about it.

Until 120 years ago, the Nez Perce tribe had occupied the Wallowa Valley, a remote area in northeastern Oregon, for thousands of years. Then the U.S. government took away their traditional homelands. In June 1997, however, the Nez Perces took ownership of 10,300 acres (4,170 ha) of former cattle-ranching land in Wallowa. Currently a wildlife habitat, the land is now used for Nez Perce cultural and spiritual events and powwows.

NEZ PERCE LITERATURE

Thanks to Archie Phinney (1903–1949), much of the Nez Perce language and many of its stories have been preserved for future generations. Phinney was born on the reservation and raised as a native speaker in a traditional manner. After studies at the University of Kansas and Columbia University, he returned to the reservation and wrote books and **essays**, including a collection of traditional tribal stories.

There are several Nez Perce authors writing today. Elizabeth Wilson, a relative of Chief Joseph, writes down Nez Perce traditional stories. Dr. William S. Penn has written many books, including books of essays and short stories, as well as novels.

Contemporary Nez Perce women still practice the traditional art of basketry, for which they have always been famous. Here, one woman teaches others how to make baskets.

In 1994, he won the North American Indian Prose Award. In one of his novels, *Killing Time with Strangers,* one of the characters is a *wyakin,* or spirit helper. Joe McLellan, a teacher, has written a series of children's books. The books are about a boy and a girl (Billy and Nonie), but the main character is their teacher, Nanabosho, who is part spirit and part person.

Cornhusk Bags

Many of the Nez Perce still practice the traditional beading and weaving arts, and their cornhusk bags are highly prized. Cornhusk bags are flat carrying baskets, like wallets or purses. They were once woven of Indian **hemp,** and designs made with bear grass were woven or stitched over the hemp. This bag, which can be large or small, was traditionally used to hold dried meat, roots, and other household goods. Some bags were woven so tightly they could even hold water. After the missionaries came and taught the Nez Perces to grow corn, cornhusks were used instead of bear grass for the decoration on the woven bags. Cornhusks were easier to work with than bear grass and are still used today.

Nez Perce basket makers still weave traditional hats, cornhusk bags, and containers from dried plants. Nez Perces who practice these arts today often sell their beautiful creations.

Chapter 5

PROTECTING FISH POPULATIONS

For centuries, one of the most important natural resources for the Nez Perces has been the fish in the Columbia River system. Today the Nez Perce tribal fisheries department employs more than two hundred people. In recent years, the Nez Perce people have gone to court to protect their fishing rights so they can continue to fish where they used to fish and use traditional net fishing methods. They have established the right to hunt, fish, and gather on 10,000 acres (4,000 ha) of their traditional lands, some of which are not tribally owned.

In 1977, the Nez Perces joined with the Yakima, Warmsprings, and Umatilla tribes to form the Columbia River Inter-Tribal Fisheries Commission. In the 1990s, the commission developed projects to restore the salmon and steelhead trout runs in the Columbia River Basin. These species of fish have declined because of loss of habitat, poor water quality, and overfishing.

Every year since before people arrived in North America, many thousands of salmon have migrated from the Pacific Ocean back to the Clearwater River system to breed. Today, the Nez Perces are helping the salmon survive and flourish.

The Nez Perce people still teach their children the "old ways."
Here, the children's first kill and first root gathering are celebrated.

In 2002, the Nez Perce Tribal **Hatchery** was opened in
Cherrylane, Idaho, to improve fish stocks in the rivers. In the
hatchery, the Nez Perces raise young salmon and later release
them into streams in the Clearwater River system. Everything in
the hatchery is designed to mimic the natural river habitat, from
rocky pond beds with logs to hide under to water flows that
vary in pace and strength. In 2010, record numbers of salmon
returned from the Pacific Ocean to spawn near the hatchery.

AN ANCIENT CULTURE IN MODERN TIMES

The Nez Perces today are a strong and growing Native American
nation. They use traditional strengths, such as a committee form
of leadership, to build a community that works in the modern
world. The Young Horseman Project also uses a traditional focus
to prepare youth for modern life. By looking both to the past
and the future, the Nez Perce people will survive as a nation.

TIMELINE

1700s	Nez Perce people acquire horses and become buffalo hunters on the Plains; they raise and train horses and build a trading empire.
1800	Nez Perce people number six thousand.
1805	Nez Perce people meet Lewis and Clark.
1832	Chief Joseph is born.
1836	Henry Spalding begins a Christian mission at Lapwai in present-day Idaho.
1846–1847	White settlers on the Oregon Trail bring diseases, such as smallpox and measles, which kill many Nez Perces.
1847	Some Nez Perces attack the Lapwai mission.
1855	Walla Walla Treaty Council; the Nez Perces sign a treaty with the United States giving up their traditional lands for a reservation.
1861	Gold is discovered on the Nez Perce reservation; settlers and miners move in.
1863	New "Thief Treaty" cuts the Nez Perce reservation to one-tenth of its original size; Nez Perce bands in the Wallowa Valley refuse to sign the treaty, which takes away their land.
1877	Nez Perce War. After fourteen battles, the Nez Perces surrender near the Canadian border.

1878	Nez Perce prisoners of war are sent to Oklahoma.
1885	Nez Perce people in Oklahoma return to the Lapwai and Colville reservations.
1895	Dawes Severalty Act divides up the Lapwai Reservation.
1900	Nez Perce people number seventeen hundred.
1904	Chief Joseph dies.
1923	Nez Perce Home and Farm Association is founded.
1948	Nez Perces adopt a tribal constitution, and the Nez Perce Nation is founded.
1965	Nez Perce National Historic Park is established.
1986	Nez Perce National Historic Trail is established.
1995	Nez Perces begin breeding a new type of horse.
1997	Nez Perces take ownership of large areas of cattle-ranching land.
2000	Nez Perce people number thirty-three hundred.
2001	Casino opens in Kamiah.
2002	Nez Perce Tribal Hatchery on the Clearwater River is opened to breed and rear salmon.
2010	Record numbers of chinook salmon return to the area of the Nez Perce Tribal Hatchery.

GLOSSARY

A-frame: a structure with steeply angled walls that meet at the top in the shape of an A.

accomplished: highly skilled.

ancestors: people from whom an individual or group is descended.

boarding schools: places where students must live at the school.

bred: to have chosen the male and female parents and caused them to produce offspring.

casinos: buildings that have slot machines, card games, and other gambling games.

council: a meeting of a few people who represent a larger group and decide what all of them will do.

cradleboard: a portable cradle made up of a board or frame onto which a baby is secured with blankets or bindings.

culture: the arts, beliefs, and customs that make up a people's way of life.

descendants: all of the children and children's children of an individual or group; those who come after.

discrimination: unjust treatment usually because of a person's race or sex.

eloquent: able to use words well.

endurance: the power to last a long time, to stand anything.

environment: objects and conditions all around that affect living things and communities.

essay: a short piece of writing on one subject.

expedition: a journey undertaken by a group of people, usually to explore somewhere or research something.

floodplain: the area of land beside a river or stream that is covered with water during a flood.

hatchery: a place where fish eggs can hatch safely.

hemp: a strong, tough fiber made from the stem of a tall plant.

hides: the skins of animals.

hospitable: welcoming; caring well for guests.

ice age: a period of time when the earth is very cold and lots of water in the oceans turns to ice.

irrigation: any system for watering the land to grow plants.

malaria: a disease that causes chills, high fevers, and sweating.

medicine man: a spiritual or religious leader.

migration: movement from one place to another.

mission: a church or other building where people of one religion try to teach their beliefs to people of another religion.

missionaries: people who try to teach others their religion.

official: a person who represents an organization.

offspring: the young of animals or plants; the offspring of horses are called foals.

persecution: treating someone or a certain group of people badly over a period of time.

persuasion: the ability to convince someone of something.

poverty: the state of being poor.

prejudice: dislike or injustice that is not based on reason or experience.

Presbyterian: a kind of Protestant Christian church.

reservation: land set aside by the U.S. government for specific Native American tribes to live on.

supernatural: beyond the natural world.

treaty: an agreement among nations or peoples.

tule: a type of plant that grows in swampy lowlands.

visions: things seen or experienced that are not from this world but the supernatural one; they resemble dreams, but the person is awake.

MORE RESOURCES

WEBSITES:

http://www.bigorrin.org/nez_kids.htm
Online Nez Perce Indian Fact Sheet For Kids in question and answer form with useful links.

http://www.brooklynmuseum.org/opencollection/artists/721/Nez_Perce
Photos of historic Nez Perce clothing and artifacts from the Brooklyn Museum.

http://www.cr.nps.gov/museum/exhibits/nepe/index.html#
This virtual exhibit tells the story of the Nez Perce through the objects they made and used over 10,000 years.

http://www.native-languages.org/nez.htm#language
A guide to the Nez Perce language, including vocabulary.

http://www.native-languages.org/nez-legends.htm
Many links to Nez Perce legends and traditional stories and to books on Nez Perce mythology.

www.nezperce.com/npphoto1.html
See photos of various leaders.

http://www.nezperce.org/
The Nez Perce Tribal Website.

www.nezpercehorseregistry.com
Describes the Nez Perce Horse Registry and Young Horseman Project.

http://www.nps.gov/nepe/index.htm
Website of the Nez Perce National Historical Park in Idaho, Montana, Oregon, and Washington. The park's 38 sites include many battlefields, including Big Hole National Battlefield, a U.S. memorial to the people who fought in the Nez Perce war of 1877.

www.pbs.org/weta/thewest/people/a_c/chiefjoseph.htm
A description of Chief Joseph with links to other topics in Nez Perce history.

http://www.wisdomoftheelders.org/program303.html
Eight wide-ranging radio interviews with modern Nez Perce people, including a spiritual leader, tribal historians, an artist, and a storyteller.

BOOKS:

Biskup, Agnieszka. *Thunder Rolling Down the Mountain: The Story of Chief Joseph and the Nez Perce.* Capstone Press, 2011.

Englar, Mary. *Chief Joseph: 1840–1904 (American Indian Biographies).* Blue Earth Books, 2003.

Gibson, Karen Bush. *Native American History for Kids: With 21 Activities.* Chicago Review Press, 2010.

Hopping, Lorraine Jean. *Chief Joseph: The Voice for Peace (Sterling Biographies).* Sterling, 2010.

King, David C. *First People.* DK Children, 2008.

King, David C. *The Nez Perce (First Americans).* Benchmark Books, 2007.

Murdoch, David S. *North American Indian (DK Eyewitness Books).* DK Children, 2005.

Nelson, Sharlene, and Ted Nelson. *The Nez Perce (Watts Library).* Children's Press, 2004.

O'Dell, Scott, and Elizabeth Hall. *Thunder Rolling in the Mountains.* Sandpiper, 2010.

Press, Petra. *The Nez Perce (First Reports).* Compass Point Books, 2002.

Ryan, Marla Felkins, and Linda Schmittroth. *Nez Perce: Native Peoples of the American Plateau.* Blackbirch Press, 2002.

Sutcliffe, Jane. *Chief Joseph (History Maker Bios).* Lerner Publications, 2004.

THINGS TO THINK ABOUT AND DO

YOU ARE THERE

Pretend you are a newspaper reporter in 1877. Write a short newspaper article about the Nez Perce War.

HORSES OF HISTORY

Find out more about Appaloosa horses. Draw a picture of an Appaloosa horse. What makes this horse different from other horses?

PLAY YOUR PART AT A COUNCIL

Pretend you are one of the people at the Walla Walla Treaty Council. Some of you are Nez Perce chiefs, others can be Governor Stevens, General Howard, and white settlers and miners. Debate why each of you should be able to live in the same area and come up with a solution.

WHAT TO WEAR?

Draw a picture of some Nez Perce traditional clothing. Think about the steps someone would take to make this clothing, and write them down.

INDEX